Hats

Elizabeth Nonweiler

raintree

sun hat

fez

3

hijab

bonnet

5

hard hat

bandana

bamboo hat

cricket cap

leghorn hat

stocking cap

umbrella hat

kokoshnik

Interesting facts about the pictures

page 2: **Sun hats** have a brim to shade your face from the sun. They are lightweight to keep your head cool. They come in many shapes and materials. This woman's pink hat is made of straw.

page 3: A **fez** is a felt hat in the shape of a cylinder worn by men in many parts of the world. They are not meant as protection from the sun or rain, but they look smart. This man is wearing a Turkish fez with a tassel.

page 4: A **hijab** is a traditional scarf worn by Muslim women to cover their head and neck. Muslim girls often begin to wear hijab when they are about 12 years old.

page 5: **Bonnets** are hats that were worn in the past, mostly by women and girls. Now they are worn mainly by babies to keep their heads warm. This baby is wearing a knitted bonnet.

page 6: **Hard hats** are helmets of metal or plastic for protecting you in places where your head might get injured. This man is checking the plans on a building site where building materials or tools might fall.

page 7: A **bandana** is a piece of cloth you can tie around your head. It can keep your hair away from your face, or stop perspiration from going into your eyes. Some people wear them just to look great.

page 8: A **bamboo hat** is made from bamboo straw in the shape of a cone, with a piece of cloth to tie under the chin. This women is picking tea leaves in a field. Her hat protects her from the hot sun.

page 9: A **cricket cap** is a soft hat worn by cricket players. The rim at the front keeps the sunlight away from the player's eyes. This means he can see clearly when batting, aiming for the wicket or following the path of the ball.

page 10: **Leghorn hats** are made of straw from wheat grown in Leghorn in Italy. They can be any shape or size, for men or for women. This man is wearing a leghorn with a flat top, a ribbon and a rim to keep off the sun.

page 11: A **stocking cap** is a tight-fitting knitted hat to keep your head warm in cold weather. Stocking hats like the one worn by this girl are also called bobble hats, because of the bobble on top.

page 12: An **umbrella hat** protects you from sun or rain, hands-free. It can be useful for gardeners, cyclists, walkers, shoppers, manual workers and wheelchair users, who need both hands in the rain.

page 13: A **kokoshnik** is a traditional headdress worn by Russian women. It is tied in a bow at the back with long thick ribbons. It may be decorated with pearls and gold thread.

Letter-sound correspondences

Level 1 books cover the following letter-sound correspondences.
Letter-sound correspondences highlighted in green can be found
in this book.

<u>a</u>nt	<u>b</u>ig	<u>c</u>at	<u>d</u>og	<u>e</u>gg	<u>f</u>ish	<u>g</u>et	<u>h</u>ot	<u>i</u>t
<u>j</u>et	<u>k</u>ey	<u>l</u>et	<u>m</u>an	<u>n</u>ut	<u>o</u>ff	<u>p</u>an	**qu**een	<u>r</u>un
<u>s</u>un	<u>t</u>ap	<u>u</u>p	**v**an	**w**et	bo<u>x</u>	**y**es	<u>z</u>oo	

du<u>ck</u>	fi<u>sh</u>	**ch**ips	si<u>ng</u>	**th**in **th**is	k<u>ee</u>p	l<u>oo</u>k m<u>oo</u>n	<u>ar</u>t	c<u>or</u>n